SOCCER MANIA

WORLD'S TOP SOCCER LEAGUES

Cara Krenn

Lerner Publications ◆ Minneapolis

Copyright © 2026 by Lerner Publishing Group, Inc.

All rights reserved. International copyright secured. No part of this book may be reproduced, stored in a retrieval system, or transmitted in any form or by any means—electronic, mechanical, photocopying, recording, or otherwise—without the prior written permission of Lerner Publishing Group, Inc., except for the inclusion of brief quotations in an acknowledged review.

Lerner Publications Company
An imprint of Lerner Publishing Group, Inc.
241 First Avenue North
Minneapolis, MN 55401 USA

For reading levels and more information, look up this title at www.lernerbooks.com.

Main body text set in Mikado. Typeface provided by HVD fonts.

Editor: Evan Villas **Designer:** Viet Chu

Library of Congress Cataloging-in-Publication Data

Names: Krenn, Cara, author.
Title: World's top soccer leagues / Cara Krenn.
Description: Minneapolis : Lerner Publications, 2026. | Series: Lerner sports rookie. Soccer mania | Includes bibliographical references and index. | Audience: Ages 5-8 | Audience: Grades K-1 | Summary: "There are so many amazing soccer leagues in the world! Readers learn about the best players, thrilling rivalries, and exhilarating matchups from leagues across the globe"— Provided by publisher.
Identifiers: LCCN 2024037298 (print) | LCCN 2024037299 (ebook) | ISBN 9798765668412 (library binding) | ISBN 9798765683767 (paperback) | ISBN 9798765681251 (epub)
Subjects: LCSH: Soccer—Juvenile literature. | Soccer teams—Juvenile literature. | Soccer players—Juvenile literature. | Sports rivalries—Juvenile literature.
Classification: LCC GV943.25 .K743 2026 (print) | LCC GV943.25 (ebook) | DDC 796.334—dc23/eng/20241017

LC record available at https://lccn.loc.gov/2024037298
LC ebook record available at https://lccn.loc.gov/2024037299

Manufactured in the United States of America
2-1013187-53809-8/28/2025

Table of Contents

Leagues Ahead   4

Glossary   24
Learn More   24
Index   24

Leagues Ahead

Fans chant "Olé, Olé, Olé!"
The stadium fills with singing.
It's a big soccer match!

Soccer is very popular. There are many pro leagues. Players from around the world join different teams.

Lionel Messi

The NWSL is the top US women's league. Some teams are Seattle Reign, San Diego Wave, and Gotham FC.

INSIDE SOCCER

Kansas City built the first women's pro sports stadium.

MLS is the top US men's league. Lionel Messi and David Beckham played here.

MLS has 29 teams. LA Galaxy is one of the best.

David Beckham

The Premier League is England's best men's league. Thierry Henry and Cristiano Ronaldo played for this league.

Some Premier League teams are Manchester City, Liverpool, and Chelsea.

Cristiano Ronaldo

INSIDE SOCCER

Fans wear special outfits to show team spirit.

The WSL is England's top women's league. Players from many countries join. Some teams are Chelsea, Arsenal, and West Ham.

La Liga is Spain's top men's league. Its best teams are Real Madrid and Barcelona.

INSIDE SOCCER

Europe's best teams play in the Champions League tournament. Real Madrid has won the most times.

Première Ligue is France's top women's league. Lyon and Paris Saint-Germain are some of its best teams. Wendie Renard and Lindsey Horan play for Lyon.

Brasileirão is South America's top league. Some teams are Palmeiras, São Paulo, and Corinthians. Palmeiras won the league in 2023, their 12th time!

INSIDE SOCCER

Brazil's Maracanã Stadium is one of the best soccer stadiums. Soccer star Pelé played there.

Soccer is growing all over the world. What team would you cheer for?

Glossary

chant: to sing or say something over and over

league: a group of teams that play against one another

match: a soccer game

Learn More

DK. *Everything You Need to Know About Soccer!* DK Penguin Random House, 2024.

Gish, Ashley. *National Women's Soccer League*. Bellwether Media, 2025.

Krenn, Cara. *Most Incredible Soccer Moments*. Lerner Publications, 2026.

Index

Chelsea, 12, 14

match, 4

stadium, 4, 9, 21

tournament, 17

Photo Acknowledgments

Ezra Shaw/Getty Images, p. 5; Michael Regan/FIFA via Getty Images, p. 7; Jamie Squire/Getty Images, p. 9; Dean Treml/AFP via Getty Images, p. 11; Alex Livesey/Getty Images, p. 13; Alex Broadway/Getty Images, p. 15; Paul Ellis/AFP via Getty Images, p. 17; Martin Rose/Getty Images, p. 19; Pedro Vilela/Getty Images, p. 21; Christof Koepsel/Bongarts/Getty Images, p. 23.
Cover image: Robin Parker/Sportimage via AP
Design elements: vid64/Getty Images; boytaro Thongbun/500px/Getty Images.